ABANDONED KENTUCKY

BYGONE ECHOES OF THE BLUEGRASS STATE

JAY FARRELL

AMERICA THROUGH TIME®
ADDING COLOR TO AMERICAN HISTORY

America Through Time is an imprint of Fonthill Media LLC
www.through-time.com
office@through-time.com

Published by Arcadia Publishing by arrangement with Fonthill Media LLC
For all general information, please contact Arcadia Publishing:
Telephone: 843-853-2070
Fax: 843-853-0044
E-mail: sales@arcadiapublishing.com
For customer service and orders:
Toll-Free 1-888-313-2665

www.arcadiapublishing.com

First published 2019

ISBN 978-1-63499-169-8

Typeset in Trade Gothic 10pt on 15pt
Printed and bound in England

CONTENTS

ABOUT THE AUTHOR

JAY FARRELL is a Nashville, Tennessee, based photographer who loves photographing abandoned structures. He has a passion for utilizing his camera to share the unique, distressed beauty of abandoned homes and structures that most of the world has forgotten. Sharing his adventures with the public through authorship and blogging inspires him as much as the adventures themselves.

INTRODUCTION

The "life after people" feel to abandoned buildings—complete with rotted and caving floors, forgotten contents of yesteryear, and the overall entropy and distress—are what fuels my inspiration. There's a freedom (and a danger) of hitting the open road and exploring the backroad to seek these abandoned treasures. These structures tell a story. My goal while photographing them is to tell those stories and be their voice after they've been forgotten, sometimes for generations.

There is a process to my work. I don't force my way in or vandalize and I don't take or disturb anything. This shows a level of respect and reduces liability. These places are sometimes a hideout for squatters or vandals, which adds potential danger to the situation. It's extremely rare for me to be confronted by an heir or property owner, but it can happen. The structures are dangerous, with roofs caving in, broken glass, nails, needles, wildlife, loose boards, and weak floors. You must know what is under your feet—another reason I prefer to go with a trusted colleague if that option is available. It's eerie; there are lots of noises, creaks, and constant echoes.

This book features the work from my travels and adventures in Kentucky, exploring the narrow farm backroads that only the locals travel. I will take you with me on the journey through some of the most dilapidated structures that most people only imagine. You will enjoy an exciting mix of forlorn farmhouses, former shops and businesses, and even an 1800s built church and a little *tour de force* in a Louisville factory.

It's not for the faint of heart, but the walls always tell stories and I enjoy the adventures. In this book, I will make my audience part of the adventure. I take you up-close and personal to these tumbling structures, far deeper than the roadside view. Through my lens, you will experience the true, authentic feel of the Bluegrass State. I hope you enjoy it!

Take only pictures, leave only footprints. [*Illustration by Kelly J. King*]

1

THE INTERSECTION

In the middle of a busy fall wedding photography season, I need to take little breaks to find inspiration and a temporary relief from the busy city. There is no better way to do that than to explore Kentucky backroads, looking for abandoned buildings. I was going to Bowling Green that evening to have dinner with friends, so I left early and allowed some time for my exploration beforehand. I made the journey to Hart County on a slightly chilly and windy afternoon to see if anything spoke to me. As usual, I picked a random direction after exiting the highway and got to work.

I approached an intersection that had two abandoned buildings across the road from one another. The area was reminiscent of a ghost town with only cars and trucks passing by, but nowhere to stop. First, I visited what used to be a large general store. Sadly, there was no way in, but I probably couldn't have seen inside the building anyhow. This intersection was a classic example of small-town Americana.

The old general store that once sold many cold Coca-Colas.

I love this very old Coke mural. This is something you don't see unless exploring on the road less traveled.

The barn behind the old-time shop may have been a fix-it shop, or used for storage.

The back side of the building—every angle was boarded up.

Above: Old front entrance doors that were weathered, but still kissed by the sun.

Left: An old industrial conveyor leaned up against the barn.

Across the road was an old gas station and corner store. I loved the country charm this old gem had, even though my inside access was limited. I certainly didn't walk away without being able to tell a well-rounded story through photos.

Findings like this are nostalgic and rare—a true flashback to a different era gone by. Society changes, technology progresses. We have to be part of the positive changes in the world and not be resentful Luddites. However, photos like this should serve as a reminder to support small local business so they don't end up in my books. Small independent business gives America a lot of the character it's known for.

The street view of this old filling station. I only wonder what the sign used to say.

It looks like they fixed more than just car and truck tires.

Above left: Off to the side, in the ground basement level as the property graded down, I saw this old bench that probably sat in the front, and an old Pepsi cooler. Now the story of this place is coming together. This was like the fix-it shop they used.

Above right: Close-up distress and patina on the siding and the window, down to every crackle in the paint.

Left: Great perspective of the sun peeking through the old-time steel gutter and siding in disrepair.

2

THE CONTRADICTION

After exploring more backroads and navigating the area, I saw a small white house surrounded by some very tall overgrowth, down a ravine. You could barely see the house because of all the wild vegetation that looked like it had been taking over for years. I almost missed this very intriguing find, just because it was so well concealed. There was still driveway access leading to the property, but getting to that house proved to be very difficult. I could barely get a clear shot of the exterior. Several thorn bushes and pine trees later, I made it to the house. I could tell it was in disrepair and I felt confident it wasn't an active dope house because of how hard it was to get to.

After walking out of the house, I started putting clues together. Something about this house didn't make sense. The overgrown and battered exterior didn't match the practically untouched, yet dated, interior. Upon my exit, I saw an electric meter still hooked up! It was the digital kind, which was a modern design to the time. It would stand to reason that if the power was cut off, the utility company would have removed the meter, unless they were deterred by the tall weeds, or didn't want to risk being bitten by ticks or snakes. Yet, I was okay with the risk.

My main focus while my writing about these experiences is sharing with my audience—making them feel like they are part of the adventure. Many people pass by houses like this daily, but have no idea what lurks inside. Some pay no mind to it. Others find it interesting and admire from a distance. Approaching the unknown is nerve-racking and dangerous to most people, and for good reason. That was all the excitement I needed for one day. It was time to drive to Bowling Green to have dinner with my friends, after picking a large quantity of briers from my clothes (even my shoelaces).

The view from the street. I don't know how to describe in words how tall the weeds and wild bushes were, without this visual.

The back entrance of the house was the only one I could get to, and even that was a project.

I don't recall seeing the entrance of a house going into a bedroom before, but that's what we have here.

The kitchen was as dated as the bedroom, but nothing about this house was typical of most abandoned houses I've been in. It was as if someone left it and no vagrants or vandals occupied it.

The living room screamed "Granny's parlor" or 1970s budget motel room.

It's startling to think that someone actually chose *that* wallpaper—the architectural version of a leisure suit or mullet hairstyle.

Besides evidence of mice, this old gas range wasn't very dirty. Someone just left this house, under whichever circumstance, and time has started taking it over.

After exiting the house, thinking something about this place doesn't add up, I couldn't ignore this weathered siding/metal awning and gutters suffering the effects of Father Time.

3

COUNTRY COOKING

On a previous trip to Kentucky, I spotted an abandoned house nestled in the weeds, but due to time constraints, I couldn't stop. It was located on the same road where my friend lives, so I knew I'd return soon again. I asked him if he knew about it, as it was down the road a few miles from him. He happened to know the owner, who told him that it was a former meth house. The renters who occupied the house were arrested for manufacturing or using methamphetamine there. It was sitting vacant for years.

Now my curiosity was piqued even more. Several weeks later, I took a breather from the grind and returned to Kentucky to visit my friend, Tim. He joined me for some exploring that afternoon. I noticed one problem as I navigated through the twists and turns of the fast-paced Kentucky backroad. The driveway leading to this house had also suffered the effects of nature's takeover. The pull-off from that very dangerous road was iffy for a car. Carefully, I pulled off and hoped my luck didn't run out getting back out. Every thorn bush known to mankind found me as I walked towards the house.

The whole package. Debris, disrepair inside and out, and a complete life-after-people feel.

I knew this place would be an obstacle course when entering. There was crunching under my feet and plenty of stuff left behind.

This isn't the worst housekeeping I've seen, but it's up there with the second worst.

Sometimes you can come out of the shower dirtier than you went in.

How sweet, kids' toys, a mural, and window wrapping with mold.

This is a first. A creepy dinosaur wall painting amongst broken toys and flop house litter.

The plastic window wrap and climbing over a bunch of crap seemed to be the common theme in this house. The living room is slightly untidy.

Mattresses! I knew it! Now my findings were complete.

That small box on top of the TV is an old battery backup system. That way they could watch their 1980s TV and VHS tapes in the event of a power outage. Life is good.

On the way back out, the little breezeway next to the kitchen sported some furniture and a rusty SpaghettiOs can.

Above: I've said it before, and I'll say it again. It's hard to resist photographing garbage, as it's part of the ambience.

Left: I didn't expect to find a manual water spigot here—they're usually on farms.

The roadside view, through many thorns.

This could be a random artistic photo. Or if you read into it deeper, it could tell a tale of tragedy.

To my surprise, I did not see any obvious clues that this house was used as a meth lab. It's possible that evidence was seized by police. Often in former meth houses, you will find many unfinished projects, but there was none of that either. Then again, there wasn't one clean inch of floor showing, as the house was loaded with junk from top to bottom: garbage, clothing, children's toys, all as if someone walked away and maybe squatters took over for a while. It was an intriguing stop, with a balance of mystique and tragedy, knowing some of its history. Sometimes good people fall into traps, and sadly children are sometimes involved. Now, this house has a voice, documented for eternity. I'm also happy to report that I got back on the road without incident.

4

THE FORSAKEN FARMHOUSE

After leaving the defunct meth house, we continued up the road that was loaded with narrow stretches, S-curves, and hills, closely resembling a roller coaster. As I traveled west into Butler County, I was observing a different landscape. There were barren stretches of road and wide-open land with only the horizon line in the background of many fields. Open farmland, houses, country churches, and a few small stores along the way were all that were in the vicinity.

Suddenly, I spotted a very old farmhouse sitting in a barren field with weathered wooden siding and fallen roofing, loaded with antebellum-era charm. Lo and behold, there was a no trespassing sign and padlock on the front door. The land was wide open, and I had this feeling that even if I didn't see anyone, they saw me. I was able to sneak the camera through a couple busted panes of window, but didn't get inside. Because of the historical charm and quality workmanship of this antique farmhouse, it was a worthy stop and a rare find.

I could see someone approaching this wonderful farmhouse with a suitcase packed and saying "I'm home." But they're far too late now.

A closer look, with structural decay and an aging air conditioner.

Native limestone chimney and weathered wooden siding, a nice contrast.

I like playing with composition and light, as well as dimension.

A close view of the decaying porch roof, and trees entering their seasonal dormancy.

An empty living room with possible ship lap wallboards and an antique upright piano was a bit random.

Looks like Colonel Mustard found his stove behind the house.

One of the rooms connected to the back breezeway.

I love this. Decaying wood and fallen roofing tin kissed the late afternoon sun, creating perfect entropic art.

We had about one hour of daylight left. The sun had this magical softness and warm glow, creating an inviting setting to continue my exploration a bit longer through the backroads of rural Kentucky. Part of the fun is picking random backroads to turn down and seeing what they have to offer. Sometimes it's nothing, while other times it's a scenic view or abandoned treasure. It is always a relaxing adventure and there are always discoveries waiting.

5

SHADOW IN THE VALLEY

Muhlenberg County, Kentucky, was in the back of my mind, as I desired to eventually explore more of Western Kentucky. The week before I made the journey, I was sitting at my favorite local hot chicken restaurant, Hattie B's. One of the songs playing over their speakers was John Prine's song, "Paradise":

> Daddy won't you take me back to Muhlenberg County, down by the Green River where Paradise lay. Well, I'm sorry my son, but you're too late in asking. Mr. Peabody's coal train has hauled it away.

I'm not an impulsive person, but this song caught my attention. I do believe in signs, this was one, and I knew it. As days passed, I felt compelled to explore Muhlenberg County for some abandoned treasures and to enjoy an inspiring day trip. Muhlenberg County is a Western Kentucky county, known for strip coal mining from open pits and mountain surfaces. Coal is the backbone of many communities for jobs, heat, and electricity. Though those benefits, and harmful effects alike, have been on the decline from its heyday.

On an early December morning, it had been raining at home in Nashville, barely warm enough not to freeze. I wanted to explore, and ironically, the weather in Western Kentucky was clear. As I traveled North on I-65 towards Kentucky, the ice covering on the trees was surreal. While driving west towards Western Kentucky Parkway, the weather conditions became dryer and slightly warmer. There sky was overcast and there was a chill in the air—perfect weather for my mission.

When I explore these rural areas for abandoned structures, I usually work off of radar, where I use my judgment which roads to turn down. Certainly not all of them pay off. After a combination of a few different two-lanes, and narrow winding country roads, I could tell I was in a closely-knit community down in a valley. I saw a house off the road, with what looked like a huge chunk bitten out of the side of it. I found the most discreet pull-off I could find and went to work.

Structural issues, windstorm, or another act of God? Either way, this house met its own mortality.

Looking at the gap in the roof boards, that may be the next part to give way.

It's possible that this tree limb is the only support the porch roof has. I'm not even sure what to say about the mattress, except I didn't feel like taking a nap there.

My way inside was walking on two planks of wood, and the floor was not very solid.

Something tells me it hasn't been long since someone sat on that couch.

This degree of yard debris is something you don't see in the city. I suppose in the country, some see it as character. I can go along with that.

Wallpaper is personal taste, I know. Someone's taste happened to be bad. Dogs at a neighboring house were barking to alert their master a stranger was lurking. I got what I needed, it was time to move on to the next.

6

SPLIT IT DOWN THE MIDDLE

The twists and turns, ups and downs, houses and farms where families settle, and disabled cars in front yards are just a few sensory details of this adventure. Winter had set in, the leaves were off the trees, and the cloud cover created an optimal dark mood. All the elements were in place and I was inspired. To clarify, I don't stop at every abandoned house/building I see. I have to deem it interesting enough to justify the risks that come with the territory of abandoned building photography. Usually, those instincts are right.

I spotted an average abandoned house sitting back from the road in a field. I was considering stopping, but my decision to make the stop was based on a second house down the bluff from this house. It was literally broken in half, like you would see in cartoons. Now my interest was piqued. There were no nearby neighboring houses, and it was remotely located from civilization as many know it. When walking across tall weeds or through thick overgrowth to gain access to these abandoned properties, it's impossible to be completely quiet. Or to not get stuck by thorns or briers.

Lessons I learned early on: never wear shorts, never wear fragile or perfect clothing, keep your wits about you, and be ready for anything. Also, be efficient and don't exhaust resources. Finish and get to the next place, if there is one. If I don't find a place interesting, I don't stop in the first place. I'd rather find fewer really interesting or unique places than more places that I'm not passionate about. It takes many wrong turns before finding the right one, but quality prevails.

The house on higher ground.

The broken house down the hill. There was only a pile of fallen boards inside. The asphalt siding was popular in the 1940s and 1950s, just to provide a timeline clue.

The side of the main house. I knew I needed to focus on the inside, but the completely dilapidated house down the hill had my attention first.

You want to see the inside? This is it.

The porch on the fallen house down the hill.

The back side of the house with some fancy horticulture.

Above left: Come on in, the door is open. I don't think those words have been said there in the past couple decades at least.

Above right: Entering the main house atop the hill. It was nice of them to offer me a seat, but I didn't want to get raccoon guano on my clothes or car seat.

I'd say this was the kitchen. The only room in the house that warranted a photo.

Looking behind the house, there was an old falling barn and a slew of debris.

The barn certainly had character. After battling the tall brush to get to it, I saw that there was nothing in it. Win some, lose some, but you never know until you look.

7

MORRIS'S GROCERY

It was ironic that I came to Paradise Rd. while gallivanting the backroads of Muhlenberg County. I thought of the song and decided to navigate the narrow farm road. Eventually, I ended up in Greenville, the county seat, through a charming town square area. It was interesting to see, but ultimately not what I was looking for. On my way back out of town, into desolation, I spotted an old storefront. The marker sign identifies the quaint old general store as Morris's Grocery store, open from 1942 to 1960. I'm not sure how the Jesus references fit into this equation, but it's the random things that make these adventures interesting. It was definitely worth a short and sweet stop.

Salt doesn't go bad, they say. Other than that, I'd say any remaining groceries would be out of date.

These are probably existing shelves used in the store. I love the color and distressed paint/wood. Let's not overlook the flower power mattress in the corner.

The building is growing a beard.

8

VICTORIAN MAN CAVE

On a long stretch of two-lane highway, I kept my eye peeled for any potentially promising backroads. I saw some houses on a narrow road that branched off, some of which had many cars and trucks in the front yard, but all lived in. Soon after I turned in, I saw a road sign that said "county maintenance ends," which should give you an idea how remote this road is. My jaw hit the floor when I spotted this very old abandoned Victorian-era house with an antique tractor in front of it. There was a house next to it, and a house behind it, both occupied. My first instinct is never to approach people or ask for permission to photograph any property—especially in an area where residents aren't used to seeing many outsiders.

I photographed some of the outside of this amazing work of art, and was getting up the nerve to approach the homeowner behind it. Rustling through brush and tall weeds, I could only be so discreet. I saw the neighbor next door outside investigating, and I caught his attention. Since I wasn't avoiding him, he was receptive to talking with me. He saw the camera around my neck, and I expressed interest in photographing the old house. The man, who introduced himself as Landy, told me to ask his brother, who lives behind the house. He accompanied me to the back door, and at that time, his brother's son, Joseph, just arrived and talked with us. His father wasn't home. Joseph said his dad would not mind at all if I photographed the old house.

Joseph and Landy told me that he was a retired art teacher and even has some projects stored in that house. The house had not been lived in for fifty years or more. When the man who lived there was ill and aging, neighbors, some related, helped care for him. When he passed, the house sat vacant from that point on, slowly conceding to father time and gradual takeover by mother nature.

Above: The front view of this very old house—now you see why I was willing to do what it took.

Left: Lovely ornate details of the fireplace, and layers of very old wallpaper.

That could have been the living room, but how would anyone know?

The view looking up. That's one way to get free heat in the summer and air conditioning in the winter.

Siding with similar weathering as barn wood.

These were some of the pottery projects the men told me about.

Perhaps my favorite angle and dimension of the house.

Above left: It's rare to see a screen door this old. What a magnificent find, with the remaining color and patina.

Above right: An old-fashioned man cave, perhaps?

It was random to find classic BMW motorcycles in the house. Sometimes you just never know. No matter what I see, I take the oath to leave it how I found it.

The kitchen sink is liable to be in the mix somewhere.

I never recall seeing wallpapered ceilings, but I've seen plenty of very old and awful wallpaper.

I'm fascinated by all the knick-knacks and the shelving everywhere.

Some very old archery equipment and a sinister looking sickle/saw blade. Too bad this wasn't a dungeon—it would be fitting if there was plenty of chain and rope.

A well-seasoned fireplace grate and framing.

Shadow, color, and light is everything here.

Furnishings and distressed interior, both of yesteryear.

Now I wonder how long it takes for a mattress to completely dissolve and be gutted like this one.

I don't think this tractor has plowed any fields lately. It was one of the first features of the house that caught my attention. What a stellar property, and I got to make two new friends.

9

THE DOG ATE MY HOMEWORK

Part of the therapy of going on abandoned building photography missions is being away from people. The solitude allows you to hear your own thoughts, reflect spiritually, fulfill artistic inspiration, and satisfy wanderlust. There are also occasional rewards and positive experiences as a result of unexpected events. I enjoyed meeting Joseph and Landy, and I've learned to pay close attention to what people with knowledge of an area or property tell me.

The two men were telling me about the history of the area, including the businesses that once served the community before closing. Joseph recalled an abandoned elementary school not far from where we stood, and was eager to point me in its direction. Finding an abandoned school is rare, so I was excited to explore it. Construction was beginning, to turn it into a distillery after renovations, according to Joseph. There were three buildings, all heavily posted with no trespassing signs. Video surveillance signs were also everywhere. However, not all hope was lost. It said nothing about being on the property itself.

The old elementary school, at the time of this field day, sat vacant for fifteen years. I was determined to search it all, since this was a rare find. The building farthest back on the old school grounds had the most distress and character, which I did get a look in. The rest of it was, sadly, unreachable inside. These may very well be the last photos taken of the school before the revitalization began.

They say, "Follow the buzzards." I did just that. On this building, there were probably fifteen buzzards sitting on the roof of this old school, looking down on me, waiting for me to fall over. Maybe they were picking the bones off the remains of the building.

Left: Kentucky is known for basketball, especially in college programs. You never know which college basketball stars used this hoop when they went to school here.

Below: The front side of the main school building.

Or was this the main building? Who cares—I got them all.

The back building, which was my favorite. This is the building those vultures were roosting on, off to the side. When I was on that side of the building, I must have forgotten to get photographic evidence.

Back of the school offices. The only room air conditioner must have been the principal's office.

No one at this school will be asking for an absence excuse or sending students to the principal's office. Or my old favorite: detention.

An old service road behind the school. Yes, I explored. It was a fairly barren area behind there.

Above left: How rude.

Above right: I hear you, but I'm not giving up yet. You're not the boss of me!

It looks like work has already started, but it's still the way I like it.

I knew this building was my favorite. Seeing this level of dilapidation made this a nice stop.

10

HAVOC ON THE HIGHWAY

My new local friend, Joseph, told me that if I get back on Western Kentucky Parkway and get off at the Rt. 431 exit, he knew there was at least one abandoned house. That road sounded familiar—it goes all the way to Nashville. I was instantly thinking I'd take the backroad all the way back home to Nashville to enjoy a different view. By that point in the day, I wasn't looking very hard for more places, but it never hurts to keep my eyes open just the same.

I realized that I had gotten off of the same exit upon my arrival to the area earlier that day. I just turned on the backroads before I found this next architectural disaster on the main road. Whenever I start to circle back around familiar territory, that usually means I've exhausted my resources in that area. The good thing is, from this point on, it was all forward momentum, as this was the road home.

What a death trap, but a great stop! This was a prime example of the importance of knowing what is under your feet where floors are very weak. Vinyl siding was placed over the original asbestos siding, all of which started to give way. A combination of all the structural issues probably sealed the fate of the house in the end. Or a family member of the property owner living there passed away and the house was neglected for so long, the house's number was also up. I suppose it's not eating any hay sitting there. Many people passing by may think the house outlived its usefulness, but I found a use for it. It's all about perception. One person's definition of trash is another's definition of character and an untold story.

The side view of the house, with a hasp and padlock on the door. Hope wasn't gone yet.

That rotted piece of plywood over not-so-sturdy joists was my way in. Do I take it? Of course!

There wasn't a clean inch of floor where I could see the way, but there were a few large holes. I watched my footing very closely, throughout tons of debris. I first made sure there was not a deep basement or crawl space under my feet.

Some climbing was involved. Only because I had to know if the next room was even worse.

It was the same basic level of disheveled.

It's possible that the wallpaper was stripped off the bead board walls.

What a lovely festive green to compliment the porcelain white tub.

Above left: As I made my exit, I stood under the porch for a moment, wondering how the hell I got in there, and how I was getting across that porch again. I admired the scenery of the ceiling in my moment of reflection.

Above right: Fine furnishings.

11

THE CHANCE ENCOUNTER

On the way back home, I took time to enjoy unexplored territory and just take in the sights. I had approximately one hour of daylight remaining, which would at least get me a good portion of the way home. The speed limit on the two-lane highway was slightly lower than on the interstate, but it was a more direct path, closer as the crow flies. At that juncture of the day, I was finished exploring. However, for the right place that really catches my attention, it's possible that I'd make one more stop. I was very grateful and excited after enjoying a successful day and a new adventure.

I did pass by a couple different abandoned houses that didn't really stand out or surpass any of the other structures I explored that day. As I traveled through Logan County, I saw a very old farmhouse far back in a field, with a long cul-de-sac dirt driveway leading to it. My eyes almost literally popped out of my head, and I knew that I would be kicking myself if I passed it by. I obeyed my instincts and walked down the long, partially muddy driveway with fresh tire tracks towards the house. My feet rustling across the land and a squirrel running across the field though brush were the only sounds in this lonely countryside setting. The property near the house was wooded, with many acres of flat open farmland behind it, after harvest.

If you enjoyed my Muhlenberg County adventures and photos as much as I did, I succeeded on my mission. This surprise bonus farmhouse that I wasn't even looking for certainty complimented the trip nicely. What a way to end it on a high note!

Shortly after crossing over into Tennessee, dusk set in, and so did a gentle mist, soon turning into a light rain. I might have vanished from Muhlenberg County, Kentucky, along with Mr. Peabody's coal train, but the photos prove that I was there.

The expanse of land behind the old farmhouse was definitely active, but I can guarantee this old house has not been occupied for decades.

The back view of the house, where I made my entrance, away from the view of the road. Although it would be easy to miss, I'm just thankful I saw it!

My point of entry. Looks safe—maybe.

The cupboards were bare, and there was no porridge for the bears.

A nice shade of blue to compliment the puke colored shag carpet.

Scenic front porch view, overlooking rotted fallen boards.

What an interesting find! After some research, I can tell you that this is a 1950s or 1960s console radio that probably had a turntable and cabinets for record storage.

No toilet paper holder? Other than that, it all seems Kosher.

Old beer and chemical containers, part of every household decor.

Above left: By far the most structurally dangerous room of the house. Also, my favorite.

Above right: Windows to the soul. This could be the perfect wall art piece.

12

SERVICE WITH A SMILE

Ironically, I had a dream the night before going on this adventure about the burned down motel from my first volume of *Abandoned Kentucky*. I thought to myself, why not explore what lies beyond on old highway 31, and do some backroad exploring? I took my dog for a brisk morning walk, and shook off the cobwebs to once again explore the Bluegrass state. Destination unknown. Sometimes doing manual detective work and exploring roads that look promising, without boxing myself in, are what yields a harvest.

After passing the old burned motel, now fenced off, I entered Edmonson County, and eventually approached an interesting crumbling garage building with a neighboring storefront. It was indeed an old-time gas station with a two-bay service center. Close your eyes for a second and picture the different thoughts and sounds. You can hear the *ding-ding* sound when fuel customers run over the hose that alerts attendants they are there. It wouldn't surprise me if they had full service, including windshield washing and airing tires for customers, while getting their fuel tank filled. Cars pull up to the service station with overheating engines in the summer, a flat tire, or they may just need an oil change and lube. The store next door probably sold a lot of cold Coca-Colas and cans of motor oil.

At one time this road was busier, because there was no interstate highway, which meant more travelers and local residents needed their services. I remember as a kid having a similar gas and service station nearby. The mechanics were always nice to us, helping adjust bicycle chains or handlebars, and letting us hang around for a bit to watch their work. Maybe between a friend and I, we had enough change to buy a cold bottle of Royal Palm soda from their machine. The one thing I wish I knew about this old garage is if they had lifts, or pits to work on cars. With the floor covered by fallen roofing, there was no way to see. That's why I avoided walking around the center of the bays.

The shell is all that stands on this old gas station.

The inside wall with a fan belt rack.

The only personalized item I found, a handmade gas price sign, probably in an era where prices didn't change daily. The apostrophe wasn't necessary, but no one was there for me to tell. Maybe that wouldn't have gone over so well anyhow.

The roof caved in, and the garage doors were falling off. This happened over a period of decades as the building conceded to time.

Above left: A very old electrical box, likely scavenged.

Above right: A fallen spring from one of the garage doors, which I'm certain made a sound when it all fell.

An old electrical breaker box at the front of the building.

Don't you wonder what the back of the building looks like? Me too, a few thorn bushes and branches later. The sun peeked out for a few moments to help shed some light on the subject.

Above left: The back entrance door gave me access to the back part of the shop, since my inside access was best limited to walking near the walls. With rotted roofing covering most of the floor, I couldn't know what was under my feet. It's on a slab, but in many old garages, there were pits in the center of the bays where the mechanic could access the underneath of a car.

Above right: The window with a view of the destruction inside.

Above left: This is what a very old well pump looks like. I love photos like this. They're so industrial and raw.

Above right: An old well house behind and in between the garage and the storefront.

The storefront next to the old garage. It looks like the floor was removed as a mercy exercise, because there was a very deep basement level underneath it.

There should be a "watch your step" sign on the front of that entrance door, I think.

It's been eons since there was an open sign hanging from this door. Based on the previous photo, this is not a door you want to walk through.

Above: Final side view of the old garage.

Right: The old light that was over the gas pumps, for a visual aid in the dark. The attendant was still getting soaked in the rain, as it didn't appear there was ever a shelter there.

13

ABANDONED FAITH

My mission for this book was to provide readers with photos of locations that the mainstream commuter doesn't see on a daily basis. I wasn't looking for just any old abandoned building to fill this book, but houses and buildings that told a unique story. Finding this architectural entropy requires a lot of searching, exploring, wrong turns, time, and patience. For me, the rewards are worth the efforts.

Driving down a narrow, curvy Edmonson County, Kentucky, backroad through an unincorporated town, I spotted an old abandoned church sitting on an overgrown hilltop. This was exactly the wild card I hoped to find for this book. I love finding old abandoned churches, but they're a rare find, especially when I have inside access. The antique church pews remaining in place added another rare element to this already special and historic location.

The title of this chapter was inspired by my friend Harold, a fellow explorer of the human condition. Now it is time for some history, thanks to the editor of the *Edmonson Voice*, a local news agency. The property was donated for the purpose of building the church in 1871. It was originally a Methodist Episcopal church and remained as such until 1968. Then the church was United Methodist until 2005. Since then, ownership had changed hands twice, and it has remained vacant. It is indeed a special gem with great historical significance.

Look at this Victorian-era beauty. It has been begging for my arrival to prove to the world it's still relevant.

Above left: Yes, that's an outhouse! That would really suck in cold weather. That analogy was easy to envision, as this excursion was on a cold December day.

Above right: Raw talent built this church with very basic materials. It still stands.

Side window view. Either this was my way inside, or that door would open further. I love the warm glow from the stained-glass windows.

The main entrance where I am sure a lot of small talk took place over the generations, before the church had its last sermon.

Above left: Interesting details in the window trim, and shape of the windows.

Above right: The good news was the door opened, and I didn't have to crawl through the window and possibly get splinters. I'd have done it if I needed to though. You're welcome.

These were very old church pews that probably saw four or five generations of families.

I saw no sign of indoor plumbing, but there was an old electric meter still on the outside wall. Ceiling fans were the air conditioning in the summer, and this old Warm-Manning gas heater was the only heat the church had.

This antique upright piano had the congregation singing along on many Sundays throughout the years.

Random findings at the altar, behind the pulpit.

Nice creepy vantage point of a Sunday School room/library/nursery. There was nothing in the other room. By now, you've gotten the grand tour.

There's something so creepy about the old Jesus/biblical illustration posters. On that shelf sat a Scranton, Pennsylvania, area telephone book from 2006. This could be a clue on timeline, but with an 800-mile discrepancy. Someone got very lost.

A nice sinister view of the church. Though weathered by elements and time, the old forgotten church still seemed structurally solid.

14

SLUGGED IN LOUISVILLE

One spring afternoon, my friend Jerry Winnett and I were returning from exploring in Indiana and decided to stop in Louisville, as daylight allowed. This was my first exploration in Louisville; however, I remain fascinated and longed for future visits there. A dedicated Eastern Kentucky exploration is also in the works, which is why there are different volumes to this collection. Kentucky has become a second home for me.

The area that caught our attention most in this charming character-filled city was the old Smoketown neighborhood near downtown Louisville. The small former working-class community, now up-and-coming neighborhood, got its name because of the kilns that once operated there. The narrow streets and shotgun houses were where factory workers resided, surrounded by railroad tracks. These abandoned factory buildings are all undergoing at least partial demolition and reconstruction. Captions will reveal the findings of my research on these buildings. I hope you enjoyed this *tour de force* of Louisville and this series of my explorations in the Bluegrass State.

Above: This building next to the old Merchants Ice and Cold Storage Tower originally served as a wagon shed and bottle storage area in its Schaefer-Meyer Brewing Company days. These are my findings through a *circa*-1905 insurance map. Special thanks to Filson Historical Society in Louisville.

Left: This old tower, built in 1881 was the icehouse at Schaefer-Meyer Brewing Company, up until the prohibition era in the early 1920s. Later, the thirteen-story tower became an ice and cold storage facility, known as Merchants Ice and Cold Storage. We found it abandoned, fenced off, and boarded up with its future still to be determined.

The next block over, we walked up an old brick alley to access another old factory that parts have already been razed. The sign didn't say we couldn't walk there, so in we went.

Piles of rubble were everywhere. It appears as though it was careful demolition, and part of the building was being preserved.

After all, you cannot replace the character of an old industrial building like this. According to the history map, this factory was originally the Henry Pilcher and Sons Pipe Organ Factory. The two-story factory had many different sections for lumber storage, finishing, varnishing, drying, pipe gilding, and erecting.

All the climbing over piles of bricks was well worth the labor.

I kept thinking how I wish Nashville still had buildings like this.

Above left: I'm envisioning workers in the 1920s yelling to each other where the deliveries were made. Perhaps by train, as I suspect there were train tracks in the alley.

Above right: We finally made our way inside. It was extremely dark in most places. A high-powered flashlight is on my list for next city exploration.

There wasn't quite as much graffiti as in the old Madison Mill in Nashville, as seen in my *Abandoned Nashville* book.

Patina on the brick is brilliant, and took over a century to develop. This can't be replaced.

Dimensions and pathways, all led by the samaritans of the universe.

Above left: It does not get any more industrial than this. Louisville hasn't seen the last of me—there's always the hope of finding more.

Above right: A freight elevator raised goods to the upper level.

MORE BY JAY FARRELL

ABANDONED ALABAMA
VOLUME 1
ISBN: 978-1-63499-114-8

ABANDONED KENTUCKY
VOLUME 1
ISBN: 978-1-63499-056-1

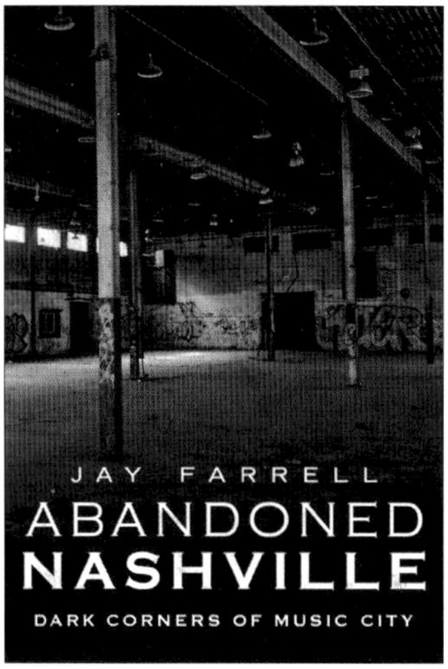

ABANDONED NASHVILLE

ISBN: 978-1-63499-113-1

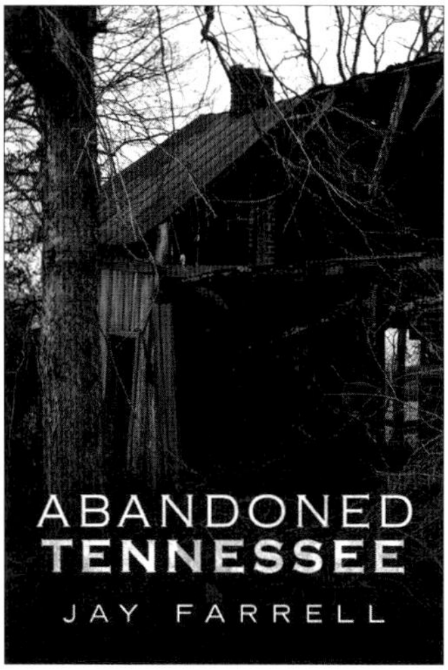

ABANDONED TENNESSEE
VOLUME 1

ISBN: 978-1-63499-055-4

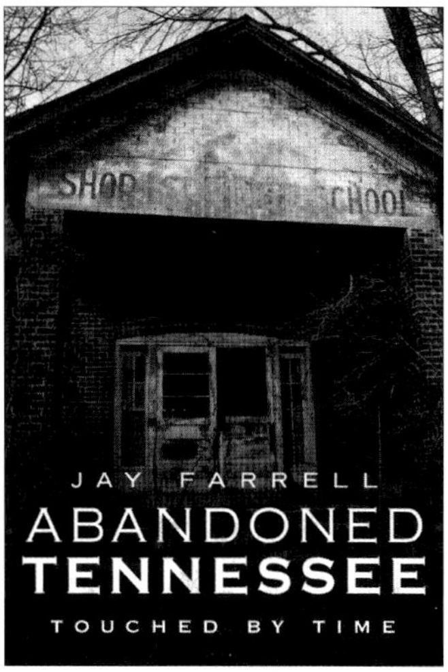

ABANDONED TENNESSEE
VOLUME 2

ISBN: 978-1-63499-102-5